Jaffa Cakes and Bubl

All rig

No part of this publication may be reproduced, stored in a retrieval system, or transmitted, in any form or by any means, electronic, mechanical, photocopying, recording, or otherwise, without the prior written permission of the presenters.

Andrea Jackson asserts the moral right to be identified as the author of this work.

Presentation by *BookLeaf Publishing*

Web: www.bookleafpub.com

E-mail: info@bookleafpub.com

ISBN: 9789357619370

First edition 2023

DEDICATION

To my two wonderful boys Theo and Jasper

To my wonderful Husband

Thank you for being my everything

ACKNOWLEDGEMENT

My amazing husband who made this experience all the more easier; looking after me and our boys so well. Thank you now and always.

My awesome family and friends for always being there, being so supportive and just generally being the best.

PREFACE

Jaffa cakes and bubbles is a collection of poems all about my experience of the birth of my second child, the initial bubble, motherhood, Big brother, the ups and downs, connections and love.

Tuesday 11th October
Making The Most Of It

Beautiful shiny day
Possible deceiving autumn sun bringing the chill
I wouldn't know, been in the cuddle bubble
Trying to take in these last precious moments
Cuddles, snuggles, idle sittings
Little things need doing but time is dear
Only this one to one time to hold him near
Poorly little eyes and a dependent demure
Wouldn't have it any other way
Laying peacefully with my arm under his head,
cried out for "Mummy cuddles" he said
I'm right here my darling, right next to you,
debating whether to sleep when there is so much
I'm to do
These co-sleep lays just you and I will becoming
to an end in the blink of an eye
Only 2 more days to go
Before you grow ever more into big brother
I admire your side profile, looks just like your
scan
I'm laying here with baby bump with whom you
go hand in hand
Although excited I'm saddened of our time
together cutting short soon to be
That's why I can't bring myself to get up you see

Laying here watching you writing my prose
You are the most precious part of my world
Our chapter will soon change, our rhythm disturbed but who knows what's to come my beautiful skylark bird.

Wednesday 12th October
The Pre Opp

The day the meeting of prep for showtime
So many thoughts and feelings
Treasured memories of the morning
Playing in the warm sunny bedroom
Tracks galore, wooden blocks
Building towers, knocking down, counting under tiny breaths
The sleep battles pressed for time
The guilt sets in for should be enjoying them
Means to a must sometimes
The jolly outlook of one can be shadowed by a more Hampered soul
The questions, the focus to stay on track
The calmness, the brightness overtakes the hasty specks
The excitement filling the body
The new paths to take
Turning the past darker, corridor days, stairwell cries, heavy hearts, shakes and waits
Into bright and cheerful merrier controlled experiences
Hopeful and wishful this continues for future days
Holding out, for one more day

One more night
One more, two more, three more comforts
Scattering around in the faith of no startle beginnings
A chance to catch our breath amongst the months of ambiguity
The restful heads listening to information so needed
To one not the other; one for control with questions,
One for go with the flow,
The questions are needed for peace of mind
Giggles at times of sweet consideration
Our relationship takes a more fluid low maintenance role
'Make sure he eats while you shower so you do not see'
The joys of fasting are yet to be
One more day before a new life is around
Whatever will be, will be bound
The calm and excitement bouncing around
The disbelief and belief surround.

Thursday 13th October
The Day Before 3 Become 4

The day before 3 become 4
A few errands to run before we chill
My emotions were high after plans didn't work
Desires for snuggle cuddles on the sofa or bed to sleep
But my boy was awake and testing mischievously
I tried to create the restful peace but instead erupt
Missing the moments of play and attention
Mum guilt sets in and a sudden need for attachment from me to him
Tears fall once again
I allow myself to sit in my feelings
Remind myself everything is heightened
Allow myself to be
To be in the present
Actually takes it all away
The power of now you could say
A wish for one last day of fun and closeness
Isn't quite the way my firstborn felt it
Remembering he could be battling with his own emotions and feelings

A new being will arrive
My explaining of my hospital visit, his grandparent's nursery pick up, mummy coming home with baby
All bound to distort, disrupt and deceiver his mood
Excitement I hope will set in for him soon
We finally succumbed to sofa snuggles and snoozes, closing my eyes letting my body and mind breath
Taking it all in once again
Smelling his hair, holding him close
The social scroll then the release of my soul
While writing this I digest and progress
My rested mind and eyes prepare once again
The excited nerves filling my body
Again the pressure to hold out one more day
Feeling of pride in my boundary setting
Enjoying the bubble of our family of three for one more day
Tomorrow the welcoming of our new team member
Or hopefully so they say
A huge smile creeps my face and my tummy waves
All is about to change again in another day
The feeling of warmth and luckiness explodes leaving my eyes teary
So very very lucky

A true feeling of looking forward to the adventure
To the future
To our family of 4
My baby awakes, his smiles and "Mummy" feel my heart
I feel refreshed with a newfound reflectiveness on our day
Wobbles are permitted I say.

Friday 14th October
Good Morning World

One of the biggest days of my life
The happiest of moments and memories
The birth of our beautiful son
Baby number 2
The team has grown
Such a beautiful day, calm and restful
Glorious skin on skin
Tiny, tiny hands resting against my face
His cheek to my cheek
Following the lion king lift
The scrunched-up body, chunky face
The pride jewels, revealing of the gender
So sure it was possibly a girl
Another boy, two mischievous scamps
A daddy vibe is felt, daddy certainly has the touch
Glistening eyes looking up in awe, listening to his cheerful voice
A natural, a caregiver, a gentle soul
Sharing the soul with Jasper, this feeling so strong
The recognition in his little face as he hears my voice
Joining them in recovery

Here we lay as a new little bond, missing big brothers amazing presence
The numbness wears off, I come around to my natural mode
Admiring and in awe of the baby we've grown
Life created one so special to hold
Treasure I'm told, the meaning of his name
Indeed my strong-gripped, loud-lunged little fella
The most amazing intense feelings surround me
His face against my arm; we lay in to the night
His little face looks up at me, we have a conversation,
Only Jasper and I understand, him with his eyes, me with mummy's voice
I will never forget that moment, taken too quick from interruption but it lies firmly in my heart
The liquid morphine is a reflective space
A dream to feel
One amazing day

Saturday 15th October
Home Sweet Home

Waking feeling amazing
Dazed still by the drugs and lack of sleep
But all of that disappears
With the precious being in my arms
His tiny, tiny body almost curled up in a ball
The birth still on his head
The smell of his being, the warmth
The love I feel
Emotions swimming around
Free to walk, but walk with care
The pain sears so much harder than the first time around
I miss my Theo, miss him hard,
Wondering how he will welcome this new arrival into his world
His little brother
Will he suddenly seem grown up
I hope not

This time it's as it should be waking up with my baby next to me
Holding him close

I'm watching the clock for breakfast, nothing new there!
Watching the clock for meds
For the morphine liquid dream
Wishing and willing I'm out today with husband and baby hand in hand

Creating a friend I hope to see again
A nursery nurse lovely as can be
Chatted galore, made me feel so comfortable and free
Free from the pain of my wound which suddenly kicked in
Reminding myself if Theo could do what he did, I can handle it
Handle it I will
The friend in the nurse helped with my feeding
Holding my son's bum up while the rest of me dragged
Where were the meds? The pain, the tears
The shivers, the sweats, set in
Struggling but watching and holding my baby Jasper close
Needing someone by side
Feeling unseen
Holding my baby closer
Desire to see the doctor as soon as can be
Let me be with my family
See my boy

I pass up the morphine dream
Wanting to feel present and seen
Not on cloud 9 although this is where my pain wishes to be
The soreness is unreal, it's so hard to move
Have to move, have to feed,
Have to be the best mummy I can be

So grateful for all I have
Still in a blissful bubble trip
Sweet sound of release
Husband appears and we can leave
Whoop sings the skylark

Snoozes in the morning, wishes of more
Excitement as we leave through the door

Air pump from nick this is how it should be
Not leaving 10 days later with a boy full of meds and troubled starts
Off we go, we are free
The day after we came in, who would believe
Mother guilt kicks in that Jasper is not fully dressed
No hat, no big furry suit… like the pictures you see.

The car pulls onto the drive

I see Theo playing calmly with nanny on the floor
I wave so big, my smile so wide
Nearly all my family by my side

Walking in seeing Theo's little face
The feelings of sorrow grapple me as I can't rush and pick him up in a massive embrace
I sit on the sofa my place for the next 12 days
The pride I feel watching Theo greet his new little bro
Daddy teary, me teary
Theo's face unsure, his eyes speak a 1000 words
Wants to cuddle me, wants to cuddle Daddy, wants to cuddle Jasper
Wants to feed on me and can't
His tears swell up so does my heart
All broken and glued in so many ways
I just want to hold him on his own, lock him in, up on my lap, cuddle him, breathe him in
But I have this new little being I want for all the same
He wants both boobs and can't and gets upset again
It's so hard I can't explain
The guilt I feel, the strain, the love all mixed into one
He kisses Jasper's head and strokes his face
My heart can't contain all these feelings

I hold back the tears
It's magical, it's madness all at once
Amazing all the same

It hadn't really sunk in that bedtimes would not be the same
As Theo crept off with daddy to his bed, weeping and crying out my name
I let the tears flow, sat crying on the sofa alone
But alone I wasn't, for in front of me lay my new gorgeous boy
Totally dependent on me in a very special way

We will settle in; I'm sure
The best thing is being home with my family of four
So it begins our new family adventure
Bring it on I can't wait, with love at the centre.

Sunday 16th October
The Bubble Begins

Waking up as a mother of two
Cosy snuggles in bed with the family
My family of four
Navigating the tandem feeding
Making sure I'm open to both
Splitting myself in two
The tiny hand on the even tinier head
'Don't worry big brother's got you'
Laying in the dim light, watching you both
My husband beside us, the best daddy he is
Always on our side

Breakfast in bed
Soreness be fed

Cuddles with my 2 days old
The time-wasting stares at that chunky face
Never a time better spent
The loveliest of days as a new team
Little one adjusting so well to the change
One day as a collective was desired and one
peaceful day was reached
Big brother setting the pace
We go at your speed

At last cuddles on the sofa with his baby bro
My eyes filled with pride
My heart grew in size
Watching you both look into each other's eyes
Your big brother so gentle, so kind
Letting you in and expanding his mind
Learning to share he gave you his cars
Sounded scared you were gone even though you weren't far
Hearing the protectiveness in his voice
I flooded with warmness knowing you both will be fine
You have each other, an older soul to look out for a younger owl
Night time guilt and emotion set in
I'm ready to let the change begin
It's lovely watching your bond with daddy grow
Just hoping this second one also goes with the flow
We will have to see outside of us 4
Visitors soon, growing their love for you more.

Monday 17th October
Showing Him Off

The first day at home with boys and visitors
Meeting all his new family
Meeting all those whose love will never end
It felt so proud to show him off
Meet his grandparents and his cousin
Aunties and more cousins
A house full
Dizzy highs and dizzy lows
Feeling like I can't breath
And yet breathing it all in like a crisp beautiful day
The slight protective feelings creeping in
Wanting only me to hold him, smell him, breathe in his newness
Have him close to my heart
His tiny little being
The squished-up bundle
Bundle of joy
Bringing happiness and pride all around
Holding him dear and near
Connections being made and tears flying
Little moments like this
Surprises and familiarities
Yet it's all new

Holding on to the older one
Sitting in the redundant wash of energy
Hanging in there with the feeling of lack of contribution I bring
Swimming in the gratefulness towards my husband
Floating around in pain from the wound
Floating higher, so very high, bubble by bubble in the love for my new baby boy
For my family of 4
For my husband, my son, my baby
The bedtime feels flooded in again
The saying goodnight, sleep tight
Setting in that the bedtime settling will no longer be me
My eyes release what's needed to try to heal that gap
Looking down
Breathing in the precious gem nestled on my lap.

Tuesday 18th October
The Birthday Boy

Thank goodness I'm more mobile today and up and around
Just thankful I'm not still hospital bound

My youngest is now my oldest, and has made his imprint firmly on the ground
2 wonderful years ago he came into the world
The early troubles you had my beautiful little boy
Amongst all the fear we still found the joy
We've had two under two for 4 short days
Today is taking away any of my pain

The magic I've found in you the last two years
There's been testing times too, bringing tears
But you are amazing with such character and flare
Now a big brother with so much care

"How is he 2 already" I hear myself say
It's been an incredible year in so many ways.
Learning to talk, your speech is amazing for a 2 year old

Singing, dancing, exploring, being bold
Running, soft plays and learning to jump
Navigating those days you've got the toddler grump
Learning your ABC…sort of, counting to 10, almost
Kicking those balls past the goalposts
Starting nursery you've taken in your stride
Sometimes emotion and tears but all things aside
You dealt with mummy having a growing bump
Becoming a big brother with so much hope

Thank you for all the fun times we've had so far
Here's a few of your favourite things, not just all those cars:
Saying no
Having a go
Tractors and trains
Puzzles, learning using your brain
Ice cream, beaches and more ice cream
Parks, daddy's van and enjoying our team
Last but not least singing happy birthday
Being your own little you in your own crazy way

Your birthday's been a day of visitors, love, cuddles and sharing
With you developing your kindness and caring
Shy of opening presents in the dawn of the day

Later ripping the paper, not letting them get away
By the end of presents galore; asking for more
No little man that's not how we roll
We have to be polite don't ya know

It's been the best, just like you!

We wouldn't have you any other way, stay special and shine bright
Our awesome singing little skylark in flight.

Wednesday 19th October
Reflections

Writing this from Memory
As the day obviously got away
I was still-fully taking everything in
Finding peace in the stillness, peace in the rest, peace in the cuddles

Big bro and daddy adventure on a splashy swim
The Midwife appointment sets up the day
All good with baby bro, all looks okay
Feeding well, but lost some weight
Catch my breath, remind myself it's completely normal so please don't hate
A restful day amongst a floor full of play
Cuddles, snuggles and family time our way

Good friends sat for dinner which felt super swell
Hanging on to my pain, I shouldn't dwell
There was something incredibly special in watching them all play
Although their age gaps could have blocked the way
Theo's inquisitive influential mind

Playing with anything and everything he can find
Swallowing it all up, the sponge that he is
Copying all that they do, jumping, swinging, till one of them gets in a tizz
Theo stands watching transfixed on their moods
While our friends wash up after our food
A nice day and a great evening until I see…

In the kind gesture of helping out and giving a hand
I discovered my hypnobirthing cards, moved and longer where they had land
Have no idea why it hit me so hard…
Took my breath away
The scruffy pile just lay
I had wanted to take them all in again, read them aloud
Now this time round was beautiful, perfect and proud
For our first birth the hypnobirthing cards were also used
Just this time round I had to be careful about what I choose
For with an elective c on the cards
The decision to hypno birth or not had been hard
Feelings released, many tears rolled
Whimpering like a baby and emotions felt out of control

Shivering into my feelings, I was totally shocked by what I found
Perhaps it triggered something from our experience the first time around
I can't explain, I just felt overwhelmed
Something in me felt vulnerable and sad
However I know it was all in the trying to help, so I felt bad

It felt intrusive, although meant in the good
I picked myself up and moved on as I knew I would
Observing; I still ask myself why it got me so hard
Exploring myself, reflecting, wanting to reach for the stars
Reminding myself to be grateful for how it all went
And only good wishes and intentions were meant.

Thursday 20th October
Adjustments

Our first outing as a family of 4
Sitting in the passenger seat seeing my baby boy drop his cars to the floor
He has moved over, for he is now the big bro
Once I'm driving again seeing him in the mirror only; is the way it will go
Noticing today little baby became more alert
All of the changes right now splitting my heart
Pain searing through, am I ready for the ride
Metaphorically I also mean with them both at my side

Sure I will be
For now I'll take care and rest
Those around me really are the best

Big brother was so good waiting to return home
Little bro had to have all his checks done

Big bro not so good in the supermarket, being pushed by daddy in the trolley, I think made him upset
This was different you see from normality
Mummy normally pushes, albeit slowly

While I was pregnant that's all I could be

Now mummy pushing little bro in the pram
All of this new, a changed little fam
Just a lot to take in for his little mind
He loves his little bro and is trying to be kind
But sometimes he melts down, confused by his soul
Trying to remember to just take it slow
For he really has taken it all in his stride
It was just him; he's welcomed little bro with pride

It felt good to get out and get some air
Big bro keen to go home, which seemed only fair
He wants to play, explore and be free
Adjusting to life as a four isn't he.

Friday 21st October
Us

Today is a different day
Been special in its own way
The oldest taken care of in the playhouse
Could spend the day with my spouse

But he is busy creating art
Making music with lyrics real smart
Happy by myself I'm ready to breath
For past days like this, on my own I do not grief
Giving me time to take in my new baby boy
My second gorgeous piece of joy
Skin on skin all day is how we roll
Going to embrace watching you grow

Lay in bed, snug as a bug
Holding you close in the tightest hug
Watch a film, catch up on my phone
Although you're quiet I'm never alone
Missing my firstborn the house so still
Precious motherhood feelings so real

The fortunate life, so lucky I see
Can't wait for my firstborn to be back to me
Erupts with singing and a smiley face

Such a cute boy with so much grace
Me and my boys cuddling together
One more grown-up, one as light as a feather
Both as precious as can be
Me and my little family

A peaceful evening with a movie and hubby
A few wakes from both babies
A perfect day, time made for kids and for me
Feeling complete, content and full of glee.

Saturday 22nd October
Being In The Now

There is no feeling quite like the fear
Fear of being unwell
Fear of leaving them all behind
Or turning it around
The fear of them being unwell
Disappearing
No longer here
Every twinge, every pain
Especially being so near
So near to major body strain
But for the most beautiful reason
Reminding myself not to panic
Overthink, blink and it's gone
Tiny one has put on weight
Tears fill the eyes and relief sweeps
Take it in, breathe it in,
Photographic memory
Remember that you may not remember
Backing up those feelings
Taking in today's feelings and moments
All the little moments
Standing out
The singing tune and blowing of candles
So close feel the heat

So beautiful to watch
Heart filled with joy
Warmed all the way through
The little face, looking up
Smiling so bright
Happy 2nd birthday again
Family time celebrations
Overwhelming feelings following a day of love
Worried that I'll be gone
Not see them grow up
Breathtaking and scary
Breathtaking beautiful, just trying to be in the moment
Have the present only
Just being now
A mum of 2.

Sunday 23rd October
Making It Count

Another day of family belated birthday fun
An even pass the parcel game, they all won

Lots of playing and squealing galore
The excitement as his cousins come through the door

Lots of yummy snacky food
All the team in a great mood

Lots of cuddles with baby number two
A chance for big brother cuddles which are far and few

A quirky game involving all
Tricky questions, everyone trying to keep it cool
The smiles again with the birthday cake
Blowing out candles like a pro, the pride he makes
Once again my cup feels incredibly full
Great memories made even for those quite small

The familiarity as bedtime rolls around
I can't stop my tears falling to the ground

Sofa cuddles are had and feeding both at the same time
He's tired, he cries, the heartaches his and mine
I miss my bedtime snuggles and his little tired fighting eyes
But for bedtime with daddy now he rarely cries,
Opens his arms outstretched for his safety daddy care
My special sofa time with my baby now, not a second to spare

Both boys asleep what another wonderful day
Making it count in our own precious ways.

Monday 24th October
Flying Solo, First Attempt!

First attempt at solo flying, both boys at my sides
Flying high
With my skylark and my Jaffa cake

Jaffa cake as his nick name is starting to be
Jaffa Jasper, Jaffa Jaspy
His big bro proclaiming 'Jasper cake' when he wants a chocolaty treat
Cup cake it used to be
A mountain of Jaffa cakes in my pregnancy see

Baby blissfully sleeping, gracing me time with my big boy
Taking my one on one time with either of them when I can
Grabbing and catching
Breaking the rules with breakie in the lounge
Felt like weeks ago, just Theo and I embracing this normality
But that feeling of a limb being missing crept on in
My new baby boy
Taking in the new, new

All of us adjusting
The new cosy snuggles on the sofa full of feeding, tantrums and cuddles
One either side, leaning on each other, squirming, wriggling looking up at me

The mobile dream, I can, but I shouldn't, but I do
Longing for the time when I'm walking freely
Stung by the guilt of wishing tiny life's away
I am right down there on the floor playing with the cars, the tracks, the buses
But the pain, it washes through, hits me here and then there
Reminds me I need to take care

While the family is out
Snacks, snuggles and sofa snoozes with the newest of our team
Till the next roll of turn
Witnessing Theo play with his nanny is everything my body needs
Looking down at my beautiful baby sleeping on me
Any wound pain vanishing away
My heart is complete and full
Warm and fluffy
The cries from baby brother bring a protective big brother close

'Oh darling' he says stroking his head
My heart growing in size
Sometimes I can't believe my eyes
Can't believe all I see and hear
The oldest so full of care
I'm so so lucky
Nicks been my saviour
I'm forever grateful to him for making this bubble so special
Helping the transition and the separation be easier for me
Providing me with the safety net
Being their safety nets
Being my arms and legs
Truly blessed for finding him
Truly blessed for being a mum of boys.

Tuesday 25th October
Adventure Time

Waiting for the midwife to come
Mayhem with the tiny ones

Checking of me is all okay, phew thank
goodness I say
Weight checking of the baby also brings relieve
The ride this time, smoother, I can't quite
believe
Little tears feel my eyes, a breath leaves my
being
The real world baby, you soon will be seeing

Soft play outing with the cousins is planned
If I couldn't go my fomo would get slammed
All jokes aside it was important to me
While pregnant we had to forgo some fun you
see
I wouldn't have been able to run round the big
soft play insides
Wouldn't be fair to Theo if he couldn't go on the
slides
So seeing his face light up with glee
Was totally everything to me
Watching him with his cousins up high flying

I did everything I could to stop myself crying
He got tired quite quickly and retreated to his ice slushy
I appreciate this poem is quite mushy
I have written some pretty serious heartfelt things
So wanted to keep this light and on the wing.

P.S Jasper's first proper fun outing, although he slept the whole time!

P.P.S First night with no more blood thinner injections whoop de whoop!

Wednesday 26th October
Feelings Within Feelings

Mum guilts kicked in
Left the blissful baby bubble maybe
Emotions still hit here and there
The safety net of my resting soon to be pulled away
The connectiveness of daddy home, our family bubble
Soon coming to an end, with ever more changes when daddy is back to work
Trying not to think about this, or overthink
Overthink the juggle
C'est la vie
Que sera sera

I can feel Theo's need for daddy more and more
So depressing to watch and to witness
Daddy leaves the room he leaves the room
Will be in daddy's company for time after time
I'll be left sitting on the sofa, babe in arm sleeping, feeling slightly redundant
Slightly kicked to the curb
Out on day release
Scared to be with me… not scared

Just different
It's all different; including, probably me
He comes home, he rushes to be with him in the kitchen
This was all reversed a few weeks back
Happy to sit by and take it all in
Be on the outskirts
Trying to sit in all these feelings and feeling okay
Reminding myself of the change Theo has adapted to lately
Reminding myself how proud I am of him

The sudden emotion earlier when feeding them both
A tear or two from me, a wobbling lip
A shiver and shake
Trying to hide the emotion but also being real to my son
The apology that it's all changed
That both boobs are no longer his
Apologies he has to wait
Apologies I roughly move him off my boob, but explain that the pain is true
He tentatively rubs my cheek
Calls the tear that's trickled down by nose a 'boogie'
The laughter from me then him breaks the emotional air surrounding us

I love him so dearly
At times so feisty like me but yet so gentle like his dad

My Creative juices flowing today
The stillness, the rest
The evening bedtime sit while I wait for husband to return from bedtime
Is enough, is all the time I need to regain and reflow those creative needs
These writings also keeping me afloat
Uplifting my creative moods
And outlet for expression; for myself to process, alongside my sons
A reflective response to the gift of life today.

Thursday 27th October
Connections

"Morning world"
"Thanks for having us again" we say
Again a taste of me alone with the boys
Breakfast is delayed for cuddles and feeding
The baby is woken by the brother … again
I don't mind really
Cuteness in the way he wants him around
Reading and playing feeding and cuddles, changes and tantrums

Jaffa cakes!
Hayo to the Jaffa cake
High-five the Jaffa cake

Watching the adventurous boy jump in the pool
Maternal mother instincts kick in
Even though I know he's in good hands
They have their own trust and games
Father and son
So let it be and enjoy watching their bond
So brave for such a young age
A lovely compliment of a 'beautiful boy'
The other lay peacefully asleep, oblivious to the noisy world around him

Observing the happiness and contentment
Safety and trust he now has with Daddy
No tears and waving of arms,
No cries for mummy when he can't see me or heads off with him
Felt so warm to know, to see
I can sit and breathe in that space created
No guilt swimming around towards daddy
A slight sense of sadness floating around near me
However I can easily splash that away
Welcome the fresh new waters we find ourselves in
His relationship with daddy renewed and reborn and wonderful to watch
Nice to make time to play this morning and make some mess
Trying to find fun in what feels like the constant 'no's 'don't do that please' 'no thank you' with the ever developing toddler
Grateful for the flash cuddles and squeezes
The reluctancy of late towards me
The following around of Daddy
So heartwarming to see
I can deal with the avoidance
He is processing, working out,
wounded perhaps
Someone else is with mummy, taking all my time

Swapping out his bedtime cuddles
Feeding on mummy when all this was his
Today saw a little insight into the opening
Letting me back in
Playing, more cuddles, more laughter

The changes of dinner time, our mummy-daddy roles swapped for now
I like the way daddy said 'your beans have run riot'
A mountain of mash

Night time cuddles when he couldn't sleep
Came running back crying and felt warmth beside me
10 mins max perhaps but was enough to scratch his itch
Enough to put his mind at ease
Enough to feel the comfort he needed
His acknowledgment voiced "that the baby needs it".… my boobs
But he gets it
Maybe that's what he needed to work through in a cuddle and clasp
Back to daddy's stronghold and bedtime routine
What a beautiful moment I just gained
Captured forever in my heart and mind
Holding, feeding, gazing up at me, a hand to my nose, a smile and a giggle

Drawing me back to an earlier moment of today's beauty:
Again a deep and intense eye lock between us,
the dark richness of his eyes, a deep connection, interlocking
Disappearing into the windows of his soul
Feeling the intimacy between us again
Holding my eldest, although only two so barely a toddler
But feels suddenly so grown up now we have a newborn
A newborn already nearly 2 weeks old
Where does it fly, like the skylarks
Amongst the rainbows, the sunshine, and fluffy clouds
At times in the rain, the thunder, the storm
But it always passes and the good times roll.

Friday 28th October
All Three Of My Amazing Boys

Nursery day comes around again so fast
The tears roll, his heart screams
'Mummy cuddles', 'Cuddles with mummy'
All the 'No's' to off to nursery we go
It's okay I tell myself
He will be okay
I know once he is in full swing he has a great day
Just the guilt sets in 'Am I doing the right thing?'
'Did I pick the right place, will he be happy?'
Is it all worth it I often wonder
He will learn and grow
Learn to explore himself and others
At least I hope

I rest the day away with my baby boy
So lazy it feels but rest I do
These small tiny times
Feeling his skin against mine
He's close, up by my neck
Floods in the memories of the hospital stay

My first skin on skin on the theatre table where I lay
Baby boy was right high up by my chin, his bloody head and crinkled face against mine
The intensities of then pairing to the intensity of the now
Almost the same,
So beautiful and cute
The faces he makes
He's growing into his face, changing so quick
Now more alert when those little eyes open
My whispering chats in the small awakening spaces
Strong little grip
Strong little legs
And a feisty feed

Go off in my mind in so many ways
Needing to stay in the present
Sneaking a kiss, not wanting to wake him up
Watching him sleep, the time fades away
Feeling his breathing on my lip
My whole body, warm and tingly, feeling content
Right where I should be
Looking forward to bathing his new little head
The stretch of his arms then of his legs
His little frown, turned upside down

Nicks worked hard cleaning the house
I wanted to spend quality time with the spouse
We laid a little chatted and laughed
Special time without interruption from little mouths
Little Jasper sleeping peacefully in my arms
Gave us space to say hello
Stop the ships in the night

Nursery comments make me so proud
"He's entertaining" Yeah hell he is!
I hear he played with a little friend and ate really well
Singing songs and coming out of his shell
These comments couldn't make me feel prouder
A world away from the overthinking of earlier

The day of bonding time escapes us
The bed so familiar by the time rolls around for sleep
The monitors movie of daddy and Theo
Enjoying their rapidly growing rapour
My heart is so full
Full from the day, full from my team

My heart just wants to hold them close but let them go into a world of dreams
Heartstrings pulled this way and that

Go my little birds and spread your wings
But not quite yet…

Saturday 29th October
The Wonders Of Life

This morning's cries break my heart
Such intense negativity approaching going to nursery
Trying to explain Mummy and Daddy will also be there
Time to explore, play, Halloween special
The cry for 'mummy cuddles' also called
The reality of this; harsh, breaks Daddy's heart not to hear
Breaks my heart to know daddy is breaking
The call sometimes heartfelt and true
Snuggly cosy cuddles be had
Often more- the sentence a comfort habitual call
The need not really there
Easily distracted
Still it cuts a deeper root with Daddy
The call is never cuddles with him
But of course it is,
It's easier to see, easier to hear from the outside
Call for cuddles with Daddy and runs off and holds him near
I could feel left out in the cold
But my love for their new built bond takes over

So proud of my boy and how he entertains
Sat created in all his glory, then reading on the mat with daddy
Small baby Jasper cradled in daddy's arms
I'm able to stand, hug in the moment, take it in
Imprint my mind forever
The sweet kind calls of goodbyes to key workers
I couldn't be prouder of the amazing boy he has become
Handled so much lately with such coolness and calmness in the bigger picture

Back home the feelings swell
Holding him close for his afternoon nap
Feeling his warmth and body next to mine
Breathing in the smell of his hair
He feeds, he cuddles it's comfort only but I don't mind
Again try and take it all in, watching his eyes as they rock and rock slowly to sleep
His body laying curled next to mine
I hold him and watch him for a few short seconds before I'm greeted with a hungry baby
I'll take those few sweet moments and first fall asleep on me in what feels like forever even though it's only a few short weeks
A few short weeks and he has adapted so well

My beautiful boy
Now your beautiful brother needs me more
Wishing I could lay watching him in his slumber

The news of impending ending of life of a friend
from the past
Very very sad
Reminds you of how precious life is
A precious thread that can come unraveled at
any time
A golden thread
Through which to breath
To keep the calm
To keep the clear
Unused
Never to be used again
Who would know

The joy of time with friends
Moods high and maintenance low
The highs in seeing all the kids play
The teachings of 'No' and 'Don't hit' slowly
sinking in
It's working, something is working
Perhaps we are getting this parenthood game
right
Are we winning
Isn't the joy in taking part

Meltdowns and laughter
Trying to join in
When the pain sears
Little minds can't contain their pain
Their love, their all
Are they enjoying taking part?
Cuddles, tears, the clouds of the last days with daddy fill the air
Don't rain on us yet
We will walk together through it all anyway… as we always do.

Sunday 30th October
Halloween Special

Father-son time at soft play
Little babe won't sleep but all will be okay
Would have loved to have gone but appointments await
However for this bonding time is great
Discharged from midwife and baby back up to birth weight
Relief leaves my body and delight becomes my mate

Our last day with daddy home
Can't believe how quick our family holiday bubble has flown
The morning seems a little fraught the "back to work" looming in the air
Hormones high from feeding them both, over worrying but reminds me how much I care
Thoughts swirl my mind
I have got to be kind

Kind to myself, kind to my oldest boy
I worry my stress and sternness will destroy
Small little minds so confusing and strong
So worried I'm getting motherhood wrong

At times it's blissfully sweet
Other times the demands my mind cannot meet
Am I showing him the wrong way to be
Don't want him to be as feisty as me
I will always lay everything bare
As long as he knows my love is always there

The afternoon lighter with Halloween fun
Not quite dress up from everyone!
The little ones looking so great, and playing so sweet
Lots of food consumed and plenty of treats
No tricks this time but the trick be this
Let them run riot but always be there with a kiss
Always loud, chaotic but fun in the family bubble
So grateful for this gang, try to be humble

The evening reappears, tomorrow going solo near
I will miss my husband so much, wishing to hold him near
Bedtime routine and no space for snuggles as baby in the bed
We will have stand-up cuddles instead.

Monday 31st October
The Journey Ends And Begins!

Solo flying
Soaring high
Just like my boys
The grace of the morning
Feeling so comfortable and content
Worried something will tip us over the edge
Here's just the thing… that worry is really barely a thing
Feeling at one so my mood follow steps
Always question what brings me this way
Sleep, diet, company, a good chat…
Calm and collected as the morning awakens
Playing as a three down on the floor
Mobile and pain-free
Enjoying while it last and while no feeding or moods
Then cuddles galore
Encourage a nap in Mummy and Daddy's bed
I lay peacefully with my boys
It's missing one huge important part of our puzzle
Daddy… daddy who works so hard for us all

I shimmy myself to his side of the bed
Can smell him on the pillow
I hold my boys near
One across my legs, wriggling, stretching as he does
My gorgeous squirmy Jaffa cake
My other cuddle up by side
Nestled in, clutching his cars
My world right here
Watching as his eyes slowly close, his body slowing to a still
He's finally given in
The three of us now in cosy day naps
Hopefully will be
I stroke his hair
Watch him sleep
Watch them both sleep
The feeling of my two boys asleep on me so deep
So intense, magical, amazing
In this one little moment
My whole being feels warm and complete
The precious, the crazy
How to forever hold them near
Keep them safe

The house has felt quiet, emptier without daddy near

My family of four, I just want to hold them ALL so near

So these poems are nearly coming to a close
About my journey in motherhood from one to two
About our new baby boy
My oldest, my husband, my family of four
My experience of who knew what!

My new baby boy is just the cutest
I like to watch him sleep
His little eyes, nose and chin
My chin… wahoo
Always frowning my frown,
Turn the frown upside down little dude
Unbelievable cute when awake
My little mole
My little morph
Holding head high
Content and chilled out

Theo cuddles him now by holding him up
Pulling him up, wrapping his arms around his waist
His neck into his head
Squishing so tight
The love so visible
The drop of him down

The sweet innocence of the no concept

The slight peekaboo of Jasper's personality shining through
The slight peekaboo of their relationship that could blossom
Seems today was a game changer
A couple of past scratches and gauges here and there with a jealous streak
But it feels Theo's feelings for him have grown even more
The love, the care, the worry about where he is

Now the worry is mine
To bring you both up
Make you strong, let you grow
Let you be you
I have Nick by my side through it all
Thank my stars every day
My experience grown,
I'm sure I've changed again evermore
But I am truly blessed with my now family of four.

Milton Keynes UK
Ingram Content Group UK Ltd.
UKHW012311160324
439511UK00013B/366